CW00730973

THE

PUB SHEDS UK

THE OFFICIAL GUIDE 2015

THE OFFICIAL GUIDE 2015

Copyright © 2015 Christopher Mark Stokes

Copyright © Mike Bacon

Copyright © Pub Sheds UK

1

First edition published in 2015

All photographs and information regarding individual pub sheds herein have been provided by their respective owners and may not be reproduced without the owner's permission.

Conditions of Sale

This book is sold subject to the condition that it shall not, by the way of trade or otherwise be lent, resold, hired out or otherwise circulated without the authors prior written consent in any form of binding or cover than which it is published.

RAISING A GLASS TO
PUB SHEDS

THE OFFICIAL GUIDE 2015

CONTENTS

A:

B:

C:

D:

THE *PUB SHEDS UK* A-Z

E:

F:

G:

H:

I:

J:

THE *PUB SHEDS UK* A-Z

O:

P:

Q:

R:

S:

THE *PUB SHEDS UK* A-Z

X:

Y:

Z:

THE OFFICIAL GUIDE 2015

AN INTRODUCTION BY CHRIS:

Welcome reader to the Pub Sheds UK official A-Z 2015. You are reading this book mainly because you have a common interest; an interest that is shared with those people you will come to see herein. Contained within this book is a selection of the best pub sheds, which have all been taken from the online community, 'Pub Sheds UK'. Each of the pub sheds have been meticulously categorized and placed in alphabetical order. We have been able to categorize them in such a way, as the pub sheds in this book are all varied and the titles given to the sheds are as equally diverse.

Myself and Mike Bacon - one half of the administrative team behind Pub Sheds UK- feel that the pub sheds showcased within this book are among the best in the UK. We feel this way about the sheds, not just because of their extravagance or characteristics, but because of the love, care and attention to detail that each shed owner has given to their pride and joy.

As most of us know, pubs are diminishing, and the free house isn't as prominent within the public social circle as it once was. This has given rise to pub sheds, and it has allowed people to unleash their creative potential upon once boring and unexceptional garden sheds. The pub sheds that we have selected will show you just what can (and already has) been achieved, when it comes to turning an empty garden space into something that can be cherished and enjoyed by family and friends. Each of the pages in this A-Z will 'shed' light (pardon the term) on the background and origins of how each pub shed was crafted, and how they were made a reality by their owners.

This book offers you a chance to grab ideas, read about fellow shed owner's and their experiences, and also some interesting stories… but most importantly, it is a book that will show- and tell - you just what can be achieved when you put your mind to it, and what a little patience and handiwork can formulate.

A note from Mike Bacon:

Pub Sheds UK was an idea I had back in February 2015 when I was a member of another pub sheds group; however, the group seemed to have a lot of American bars. So, this is when I thought, there is definitely room for us brits to have our own UK version. Not long after having the idea I asked Ian - my father in law- what would he think about starting our own group with Ian acting as the second admin. I said we could call it Pub Sheds UK, and in my eyes, all I could think about was *"Best of British"* so I decided on the union jack flag as the group's banner, with a big bold yellow font to make it very eye catching. The page finally opened in the beginning of March 2015 and now has over a 1000 members; a number which still climbs by the day. I think the group is perfect for us sheddies to give advice and help others as much as we can. However, the biggest thing I could say is, the banter is fantastic, and without the Pub Sheds UK members getting involved, we wouldn't have a group at all.

So, on behalf of me and Ian, we thank all our members and hope for lots more pub sheds- and banter- in the years to come.

Thank you once again for choosing to read the Pub Sheds UK A-Z. We hope you enjoy it.

Regards,

Chris & Mike.

THE *PUB SHEDS UK* A-Z

'IN BEER WE TRUST'

THE PUB SHEDS UK A-Z

Annabelle's

Steven Bradley, Newcastle

After serving 22 years in the Army and having an unmanageable amount of clutter, I decided I was going to have a shed/man cave to keep it all in; kind of like a little retreat where I could relive memories only a few would understand. Soon though the shed quickly became a bar where my family and friends would come and linger and indulge themselves in a few drinks and a bite to eat, whilst also using the space to enjoy each other's company. My shed is still in its infancy, so I cannot wait to start using her properly and having great party nights. The bar itself was named after my mother in law who sadly is no longer with us; she was a lovely lady who also loved a drink and a good party. She would have loved to visit this place. As her neon plaque reads: *'Annabel's; Come early, stay late, bring all you drink, drink all you bring.'*

The Ark

Lisa & Richard Nordsted, Newport Pagnell

The Ark was born following the unforeseen circumstances caused by a tree falling on my house a year ago. Following the incident my previous sheds were completely destroyed. So instead of replacing both sheds, we decided to build the one large shed. It was the day our lovely shed man Barry began the construction of our new building, that it started pouring with rain; I shouted to him "good job, you're building an Ark!" hence the name of our pub shed. As you can see from the photographs, we only have a small yard, so it felt to us as if the Ark was landing in it. Thanks to the ramifications of the falling tree, we were able to create the best little shed in Newport Pagnell.

Auld Reekie

Barry Reekie, Carnoustie Scotland

The name of my pub shed came about due to two reasons. Firstly, Auld Reekie is known to be very famous within the Scotland capital of Edinburgh; the second reason for me choosing the name is that Reekie is also my surname, so it worked perfectly. I built my pub shed bar predominately so that I could have fun and also cheap nights, which gave me a lot of laughter. The pub shed is 16 x 12 feet in size, and it has been fully insulated. The bar inside the pub shed was made from recycled wood and old pallets, and the flooring at the front of the Auld Reekie, was made from sliced trees, which only cost me around £30. Behind that flooring it is hessian, in which you can see the brown between the slats. In total it took me around 3-4 months to build, and I have to say, I love it. It also has a whiskey barrel inside which is 3ft x 3ft and it weighs around 9 stone; it is a great piece that enables me to stand around with the lads. My pub shed is located in Carnoustie which is a famous golfing town.

The Appleton Arms

Mark Appleton, St. Helens, Merseyside

The Appleton Arms was originally based upon the concept of re-kindling the experiences of growing up in different pubs during the 1970's and the early 1980's, whilst keeping it in the style of the famous "Greenall Whitley" brewery which was all started in St. Helens back in the late 1700's, before moving its brewery and distilling empire to Warrington, whereby it eventually rolled over and died as a company towards the end of the 20th century. Creating something like this, in these styles also gave me the perfect opportunity to store my ever growing single malt whiskey collection. The Appleton Arms was created in tribute to my father and brother, and it contains all the elements of a traditional pub, such as a handmade wooden bar, snug area, real pub signage, a dart board and a wood burning stove. *"Whiskey, you're the devil... you're leading me astray, over the hills and mountains and to Americae. You're sweeter, stronger, decenter, and you're spunkier than Tae O Whiskey. You're my darling drunk or sober"*. The Appleton arms was also crowned Shed of the Year in 2014.

THE PUB SHEDS UK A-Z

The Blue Bar

Sharon & Dave Kilday, Oldham

My bar began as a small home bar which was located in the conservatory; however, after a while, my good lady decided that it was in the way. This meant that I had to relocate my bar, with the most suitable place seeming to be my shed. This idea resulted in me having a mass clear out of the shed before I was able to install my bar. Soon my shed became 'The Blue Bar'. It didn't stop there however, as my neighbour came to me and told me that he was getting rid of his own shed; so I procured it from him and decided to join it to my own shed, which then made the total size of my shed 11x6 feet. The idea for the name of The Blue Bar came to me when I found some cheap blue cuprinol in a local store. One of the best things to come out of having a pub shed is that I am now the easiest grandpa, father and husband to buy presents for. The only downside is that I am now running out of socks and aftershave. My favourite quote is, "24 hours in a day and 24 cans in a crate... coincidence, NO WAY!"

The Bullseye

Vicky Irvine & Steve Tidd, Southend on Sea

The concept of The Bullseye was dreamed up in the summer of 2013, when Vicky Irvine and Steve Tidd were sat in their hot tub thinking about how they could move their bar into the garden. It was after they began looking into buying a summer house and realising that they were going to be out of their budget that they had to come up with an alternative idea. So, Steve soon set about learning how to build one himself, and by October 2013 the shed was constructed and completed at the bottom of their garden. The finished creation boasts a sizable variety of drinks and often hosts regular football, boxing and casino nights along with ladies cheese and cocktail nights. As well as its large variety of alcohols which have origins from all around the globe, The Bullseye also allows you to enjoy its free Wi-Fi connection, an unlimited jukebox, pool table, fruit machine and a darts board. To accompany all this, roulette, poker and black jack can also be arranged with advanced notice. The Bullseye got its name from the fact that Steve is an avid darts player. The Bullseye pub shed has also been featured in one national newspaper, the local newspaper, and it also has one important celebrity fan… Jim Bowen!

Bar Star'D

Warren Turfrey, West Yorkshire

A few years ago I decided that it was time to start entertaining my friends during the summer months. After many years of being entertained at other peoples BBQ's and after having my first summer with just a gazebo up, I decided I wanted something different for the following year. That something different, came in the form of my very own pub shed. I built the pub shed myself trying to use as many "used" materials as I possibly could. I created the bar and added double glazing and a UPVC door. Inside the pub, I added a bar with light up pumps and a window which was originally a table top. The name of the bar was something which both, me and my son Ryan came up with; it was the first time that we had really given thought to a name for the pub shed, and we eventually stayed with the name Bar Star'D. The shed is now used by me and my mates and it is a place where we can enjoy drinks and exchange banter.

Badly Shed Darts

Paul Doyle, Liverpool

Badly Shed Darts, was created as a pub shed, and was fully furnished with a bar, dartboard, projector and a drum kit. The pub shed also includes a seating area which is accompanied by disco lights and lasers. The pub shed even has its own internet connection. The name for the pub shed was created as a joke, taking the same design as PDC (Professional Darts Corporation) and BDO (British Darts Organisation) hence the name of my pub shed becoming BSD, which stands for (Badly Shed Darts). We came up with this name as our throwing wasn't quite up to the same standards as the other two popular darts organisations. Badly Shed Darts is always open…. especially on a Friday evening.

THE PUB SHEDS UK A-Z

The Chosen Man
James Edmond Cullen, Moreton, Wirral

The Chosen Man is a friendly and dedicated pub shed located in Moreton in the Wirral just off the M53. It is a location where only the chosen few are usually invited. At The Chosen Man pub shed, you get to remember those who have served our country, and it was given its name in honour of the regiment in which the pub shed owner served with; The Royal Green Jackets, "Sharpe".

Coco Jimbo's

Jim Gillespie, Falkirk Scotland

I always wanted a 'Wee' bar out the back. It was whilst we were on our holiday in Mexico that I kept mentioning it to my brother in law, and asking him consistently, if he would help me build one. During our holiday we visited a place called Coco Bongos, and that's when the idea- and the name- for "Coco Jimbo's" struck me. From there the creation of my very own pub shed took form, and it is now a place that we are able to have recurrent get-togethers. We have also had many various card schools; I usually partake in these with the lads from work. My pub shed is located in Camelon in Falkirk Scotland.

The Cave

Jason Barber, Swaffham Norfolk

The Cave, was given its name when friends began to nickname it; the title then stuck and it has been known as such ever since. The Cave is a pub shed that has been built, as a place where my family and friends can gather and relax in one another's company. The cave has also become a place where I am able to chill out after work and indulge myself with a nice cold pint of my very own homebrew, whilst also listening to music on the jukebox. The pub shed was entirely hand built by myself, with its six doors all having been purchased on eBay for just £120.

The Cock Inn

Wayne & Becki Livesey, Bolton

The Cock Inn pub shed has been completely hand built by myself. It has been constructed predominantly with the use of reclaimed wood; and even the doors of the pub shed were handmade. When building my very own pub shed, I tried to continue the theme of an old English style pub on the outside, and I have also recently added a beer garden. Inside The Cock Inn, we again tried to create the theme of an old English style pub, and we used more reclaimed wood to build the beams, the walls and even the bench. The remaining furniture we managed to acquire from an old Bolton pub that was in the process of being demolished. To decorate our pub shed we managed to locate many items of pub memorabilia from various breweries, car boot sales and even auctions. As for the bar itself, I have to say that it is my pride and joy, as it has been crafted from old tree logs, old wardrobes and the floor was made from the wood left behind from an old garden shed. The back of the bar was then made from an 1872 church organ surround that was kindly given to me by a church that was being renovated; I kept the organists mirror attached to hold on to a tiny piece of history.

THE **PUB SHEDS UK** A-Z

The Dug Hoose

Craig & Terri Hall, Kirkcaldy, Fife Scotland

The Dug Hoose began as an idea that was merely in my head; that was until my wife gave me a cause to do it. We wanted to get it completed and ready in time to have a family barbeque. So -soon after- the challenge was on, and I began work on getting The Dug Hoose started. I already had a 10x10 foot summer house, so all I needed to do was get going on the interior. All of the interior work was carried out by myself and then finished off and decorated by my wife. The name of the pub shed, (The Dug Hoose) came about, as that's where I would have been if I had not finished the pub shed in time for the barbeque. Since its completion, we have enjoyed plenty of good times, and we hope that our new space, will offer many more good times in the future. However, even now our pub shed is not "finished" as such, as we cannot see it ever being fully finished, as there is always more you can add, and I do have plenty of ideas for extending the bar and adding to it in the years to come.

The Driftwood Bar

Dave Randle, Derby

Welcome to The Driftwood Bar. My pub shed is located in Derby and it is 8ft x 7ft in size. Originally the shed started out as a playhouse, as I had built it for my daughter. However, as she eventually came to lose interest and no longer used it, I spent many hours of my spare time browsing the Pub Sheds UK Facebook page. It was this page that starting to make me think about converting the unused playhouse, into my very own pub shed. I did give my daughter the option of either keeping the playhouse, or letting daddy convert it into a pub; and she said that I could have a pub as long as she could help behind the bar! For me it was a win-win, as I had managed to acquire both the premises and the staff already. The pub shed was named The Driftwood Bar after a bar of the same name at Pentewan Sands, which is one of my four most favoured holiday retreats; it is also coloured to match their local St. Austell brewery ale Tribute. Within only a few weeks of opening we have already enjoyed many fun nights in the shed, and it has become quite the focal point for parties with our family and friends.

The Dog House

Jay Thornton,

The Dog House pub shed was an idea that came to me when I moved into a new house last year. As I have always been a keen home brewer, I very often thought of having somewhere that I would be able to serve my own beer from. Originally, the idea started out as an ordinary and quite standard shed, which had been taken and converted into a small home pub. However, that was until my very helpful builder friend got involved in the project with me; and, the rest - as they say- is history. My simple and unexceptional shed, soon got transformed into a fifteen square meter block building that was completely clad in timber. Within my pub shed, there is a now a custom wooden bar, a log burner, fruit machine, many pieces of old pub furniture, optics, numerous fridges, and alongside all this is my projector and sound system. My pub shed has only been open for a few weeks as of yet, but already, myself, family and friends have had some great nights in there.

Double Tap Lounge

Stuart Campbell, Kilbride Scotland

The Double Tap Lounge was a pub shed that was inspired by my late mum and dad, both of whom were known to have liked a dram or two. The name of my pub shed derives from the drumming term "double tap" which is what tells the band to stop when they come to the end of the music that is being played. The double tap lounge is the best place to retreat to at the end of a hard day, and it is also often used as a regular place to hold practice sessions and to indulge in a few beers to keep us going. The Double Tap Lounge is a 12 x 10 foot pub shed and it was completed in March 2015.

THE *PUB SHEDS UK* A-Z

E

Entertainment

The main purpose for many people creating a pub shed, is so that they can enjoy them with friends and family; such as holding special events, enjoying special occasions, or simply using them to be able to indulge in a few drinks whilst listening to some music. These next few pages have been compiled to show you what people have already used their sheds for; there are Halloween parties, weddings and even Christmas dinners. A pub shed is more than just a well decorated space; it's something that becomes a part of people's lives, it's somewhere they can retreat to and get away from normality. Pub sheds are a way of putting entertainment into people's lives, and using the space they have created to spend more time together; pub sheds are now also being used as an alternative to buying function rooms for special occasions as it costs a lot less and parties feel more homely. This section will also show you that entertaining items don't have to be bought, as you can sometimes make them yourselves with one of the most popular items being the homemade jukebox. The photos you will come to see have been provided by more members from Pub Sheds UK, capturing the best moments from their time in their sheds.

Halloween:

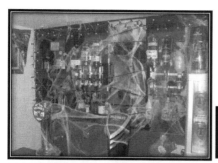

Halloween at Angels
Share – Jo-Ann Brown

Mally Davidson –
Halloween 2014

Halloween at Zee
Garage Bar 2014 –
Mathew Bradley

hen parties &
weddings

The Cock Inn Hen Party - Craig Molyneux

Ruby Wedding Anniversary – Michael Hope

CHRISTMAS

Christmas Dinner at Monas Bar – Simone Massam

Christmas 2014 – John Willmott

Christmas 2014 –Glenn Parkes

Mike Bacons Mom pulling her first ever pint at Christmas

BIRTHDAYS

Sons 21st Birthday at Angels Share - Jo-Ann Brown

40th Birthday at the Koi & Bulldog – Jenny Foster

Daughter's Birthday Party at The Priory – Gary Jackson

Best Friend Laura's 40th Birthday – Ian Humphreys

Lynn Hughes

50th Birthday

Sons 18th Birthday Party – Graham Kinkead

Chris Cowley's 58th Birthday at Funky Samples

Sports
Gatherings

FA Cup Final 2015 –
Dawn Price

World Cup at the
Tipsy Bar – Darren
Williams

64

New Year

New Year's Eve at The Jockey – Simone Massam

New Year's Eve at Georges Bar – Stuart Bird

𝕵𝖚𝖐𝖊𝖇𝖔𝖝𝖊𝖘

As well as celebrating great occasions, many people like to go to their pub sheds just to chill and listen to some music. One of the most innovative ways that pub sheddies have found to listen to their music collection is by making their own jukeboxes instead of buying one. The majority of the jukeboxes you will see in the following photos have been created using touchscreen devices which are capable of being loaded with apps that can play any music the person wishes it to. These devices have then been decorated and cased in materials such as wood or metal, before being finished with lighting, and even text to give the jukebox those extra personal touches; maybe what you see here will give you the inspiration needed to try and make your own.

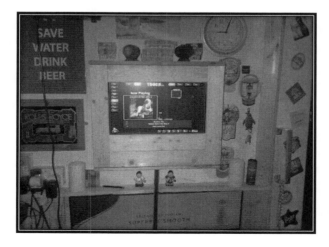

THE PUB SHEDS UK A-Z

The Frog 'N' Cat

Paul Frogncat, Desborough Northants

The Frog 'N' Cat is a place that has a great atmosphere, and it is truly a pub shed that makes any night, seem like you are having a great night out. The Frog 'N' Cat pub shed has many varied features, including: a bar with an empty fridge, a sound system, three laser lights, two LED's, one moving head, strobe and ultra violet lights, and alongside all this it even has its very own smoke machine. This pub shed also has many other essentials; ones that every pub shed requires, such as a dart board, and a BBQ. The Frog 'N' Cat also has DJ decks, along with DJ Essex Matt who is on call for our many summer parties. People who visit The Frog 'N' Cat also can't believe that it is all actually a shed, as originally it was a pigeon loft, until it was fully converted in the year 2000. My pub shed acquired its name, as the walk up toward the pub shed would often see frogs littering the pathway with cats around trying to catch them.

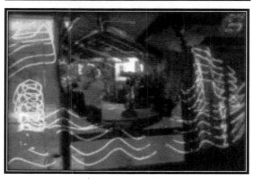

The Farmers Arms

Andy Farmer

Hello, and welcome to The Farmers Arms. I only started work on my pub shed project back in May 2015, and I used many of my days off work trying to get it completed. The pub shed is 14 x 10 feet in size and it has been fully insulated to keep it warm on those cold winter nights. The bar area in The Farmers Arms is still under construction but I'm hoping sometime soon, to get a fully working real ale pump up and running. However, even though my bar may not be at its final stage, the remainder of my pub shed has been filled with all the necessities, such as Sky TV, and a jukebox for my music, and alongside this it also has a PS3 so that I can have FIFA nights with the lads. Although there is still some left to do; I have put many hours into creating my pub shed, trying to get it looking great, and I have been able to spend a lot of time in there already; with my wife planning many parties.

The Fell Inn

Nigel Webster, Lincolnshire

The idea for The Fell Inn was born in the spring of 2015, when, after sitting outside our summer house drinking a beer, the good lady wife said, *"You could put a shelf up to display all the different Wychwood brewery glasses and bottles you've collected!"*- And that was the beginning of our pub shed. Soon, as a shelf became filled with my collection of many bottles, we decided to get a bar for the glasses. Decorating the inside of the pub shed are many beer mats adorning the ceiling, and Landrover goodies are seen covering the walls; alongside this there is also a fine collection of beer bottles. As we live in the country side, The Fell Inn is often used for small get togethers, and also to relax in. The naming of the pub shed came about due to my profession as a lumberjack, as 'Felling Trees' is a saying used often by lumberjacks for cutting trees; hence the name 'The Fell Inn' eventually coming to be the name of our pub shed; which is also followed by 'Stumble Out'.

Funky Samples

Chris Cowley, Doncaster

The Funky Samples pub shed is based around mine and my daughter Claire's music memorabilia. Both I and my daughter are the landlord and landlady of our pub shed. Funky Samples has been decorated and outfitted with everything a pub shed would need. One of the most prominent features is its very comfortable seating area which easily seats up to eight people. Funky Samples also offers guests access to the internet, and they can also watch TV or listen to music on our music system; our pub shed also has its own PC. We feel that Funky Samples is a very friendly pub shed, and we like to welcome all of our friends and family. In the future we are looking towards hopefully extending our pub shed, maybe by the end of next year; it is currently 16 x 16 feet in size... but we would love it to be bigger.

THE PUB SHEDS UK A-Z

Gardeners Arms

Toni-Ann Williams, Tintern

For the Gardeners Arms pub shed we chose a Caribbean theme, predominantly, so that when the weather is miserable, we can still dream of being in the Caribbean, whilst enjoying our time spent with family and friends. The name our pub shed was given came about due to us having a rather large garden, so for us it was very appropriate. Sometime in the near future - hopefully before the winter - we will begin work on adding a porch over our seating area, as this will allow us to use our bar in all weathers. When we are building we always make sure that we have extra wood than what we had planned for; as we usually find that when we are building, plans always tend to change. Another tip we have also found quite useful is to secure your bar into the ground if appropriate, so that even during the strongest winds, the bar will be hard to move. The Gardener's Arms is located in the lovely countryside of Tintern near Chepstow and our garden backs onto the Forest of Dean.

The Grove Bay

Barry Murphy, County Wicklow, Ireland

The Grove Bay was formally known, simply as, 'The Shed'. Having a pub shed was always a dream of mine; a dream that lasted about twenty years. It wasn't until I moved into a larger house in 2009 and finally getting a bigger garden, that my twenty year old dream, could become a reality. After a slow start in 2011, the shell of the shed was eventually completed. Two years later in 2013 following many discussions with my darling wife, Catriona, we decided to put some of our savings into the shed, and get it insulated, and have a proper floor laid. Alongside this we also had seating installed with the help of our four very good friends, Mark, Joe, Jimmy and Trevor… at long last; our shed was getting a make-over. The official launch of our pub shed came on New Year's Eve, and when family and friends packed into the shed they were amazed at how great it looked. The name for The Grove Bay came about when a neighbour gave me an old street sign, so I decided to erect a pole outside so that I could put the sign up. Overall the cost of the shed to me is priceless, and I feel it will never be truly finished; as every sheddie knows, there is always something better needed for a pub shed, and seeing things when you're out and about such as at car boot sales, will always make you want to buy them. My pub shed is 25 x 15 feet in size and it even has its own toilet and sink behind the bar.

The Grafton Arms

Mike Bacon, St. Helens, Merseyside

My name is Mike Bacon; I am from St. Helens Merseyside, and I am also the admin for Pub Sheds UK. My pub shed is called The Grafton Arms, as it was named after the well-known Grafton Club in Liverpool; and when I was a young lad, I heard many stories about Thursday nights in the famous Grafton; stories not to be repeated here. I have always had an interest in pubs, having worked as a barman and then as a relief steward in pubs and clubs in my younger days, and I always found it to be quite the buzz. Due to not having a very large garden and not having much spare space, my pub shed is 10 x 8 feet in size, yet it still has two opening windows. However, as I am not a DIY person, I was lucky enough to have the landlord of The Jockey; and also my father-in-law, Ian, to help me with my project. Nearly four years down the line, The Grafton Arms is just how I had originally imaged it. It now has working pumps connected to a cooler in a separate smaller tool shed, and alongside this it also has its own Wi-Fi, Sky TV, and of course, my homemade jukebox. As well as all this, my pub shed also has a fine collection of spirits and beers; all of which makes it the perfect place for me to watch my beloved Liverpool FC in peace with my dad. I have also been able to have some drunken nights with family in the Grafton Arms, as well as being able to spend time with friends. My future plan for my pub shed, is relocating it to a bigger garden, and expanding the size of it... so watch this space.

George's Bar

Stuart Bird, Wolverhampton

George's bar was built entirely from reclaimed wooden pallets. My pub shed has been decked out with LED lights, a sound system, a jukebox which was made by myself, an under the counter fridge, optics and many more accessories that a pub shed wouldn't be complete without. The walls of my pub shed have also been fully insulated then recovered with boards; those boards have then been decorated with many varieties of beer mat. George's Bar is 10 x 8 feet in size, with an extra meter having been built on the side, as well as a decking beer area for outside drinking. My pub shed was named after our cat, because during the time that I was building my pub shed, he was forever in it, hence the name. My pub shed can be found in Wolverhampton in the West Midlands, and it was built in 2014.

THE PUB SHEDS UK A-Z

The Hedgerow Arms

Dean Cantillon, Rownhams Southampton

Hello, my name is dean, and I am the landlord of The Hedgerow Arms, which is a pub shed based in Rownhams, Southampton. It was after I moved to a new area and seeing the local pub being closed for refurbishment; I decided, that as a way of greeting my new neighbours, I would convert my old 12 x 10 foot shed, into The Hedgerow Arms. Since opening my pub shed I have been able to meet many of my neighbours and I have been enabled to create many friendships with them. My pub shed is a great way of sharing good times with both family and friends. The Hedgerow arms was officially opened by the one and only Saints, Sunderland and Nigerian and International Reuben Agboola on the 26th June 2015.

The Hiccup Inn

Rachel Baron-Smith, Somerset

The Hiccup Inn is located in Somerset, in a small village called Hinton which is a sub village of Martock. Our pub shed acquired its name partly because it was funny, and also because of the film "How to train your Dragon." The theme of our pub shed is quite simply, everything that we love. The walls of our pub shed are covered with maps as we had lots of them and thought it would be the perfect way of wallpapering in a cost effective way. We also love natural wood so our pub shed has plentiful supplies decorating the interior. The beam in the shed was put in due to an internal wall being removed, and it had been holding up two beams on the ceiling. We coach bolted the beams together but a couple of weeks later the roof of the shed began to sag, so we installed the new post. The shed we own used to sit in the neighbours garden, and whilst the property underwent renovation we acquired the shed along with a section of their garden, as it had an asbestos and concrete roof and the developer didn't want to move it. So for us it was great, as we now had our own shed, alongside this we had a summer house, and a workshop, so we didn't need to use the shed as a potting shed, as there was a cottage plant nursery next door. So we soon began racking our brains in an attempt at finding an idea that would put the shed to good use. Ultimately we came up with the idea of turning it into a pub shed... the rest as they say, is history. We soon got to work on the shed installing a new roof over the top of the asbestos, and on the inside we insulated it and covered the walls with plaster boards. However, even after the work we have done so far our pub shed is still a work in progress, as we need to clad the outside with wood and we will also be creating an outside decking area, where there will be a space for an outdoor fire; we will also eventually have a go at making our own homebrew and get our pumps working in the shed.

Hobby's Bar

Chris Hobson, Bolton

My pub shed is called Hobby's Bar; it was given this title as it was also my late dad's nickname; Hobby's Bar is located in Bolton. I purchased a 7 x 5 foot shed from a company based in Nottingham, with the sole purpose of having it turned into a bar. Although my pub shed is not the biggest, it is still my little oasis, which allows me to get away from day to day living. As I am a patriotic person, I decided to decorate my pub shed appropriately. The interior of my shed has a trophy wall where I was able to showcase my medals which I achieved from recent runs; on the opposite side of the pub shed I have got a ticket wall which has lots of old concert, football and holiday stubs; I feel that every ticket collected tells a story. Recently I also acquired a proper pub bench which I was able to place outside my pub shed; this was great for providing extra seating. My pub shed is also used for storing my homebrew which I have found comes in rather handy. My pub shed is still a work in progress; however, in the future I am looking to add a hand pull.

Happy Shed End

Martin Denholm, Worthing West Sussex

The Happy Shed End pub shed is my pride and joy, and I had the idea for it many years ago whilst my sister lived in Africa, as over there they all had bars in their houses. When she came home they again put one in their house, and we had some brilliant nights. The trouble was we never had room at my home; at least that's what my wife said. So, I came up with the idea of having one in our garden. By now we had three kids all of an age where they would be able to enjoy it, and they kept on at me to build it, and my eldest bought me things to put in it for my 50th birthday. Eight years later I started the project after finishing some decking. From the start it was always going to be a Caribbean type shack, but once I started, it ended up becoming a pub. The panels in the front came out of a pub in Ford, and I attained them from a salvage yard. Me, and my wife's dad drink in there and we have had up to eighty people in it before now with a band to raise money for Alzheimer's, as my dad suffered with the terrible disease and passed away in 2013, along with my mum the week after. One of my best memories is my dad's face when I took him up to see it after it was completed; his face was a picture, and he loved it. In the future we are going to add a TV, and an outdoor sound system, as well as a new roof over the bar, along with a rather large blind to keep punters dry when it rains.

THE *PUB SHEDS UK* A-Z

Infinity Lounge

Steven & Dawn Parfitt, Wigan

Steven and Dawn Parfitt are the landlord and landlady of the Infinity Lounge in Wigan, Greater Manchester. When creating their pub shed, they knew that they wanted something different, and they thought that their shed would make the perfect cocktail bar and chill out lounge, for both family and the children. With the help of their teenage sons they decided to create an infinity table and infinity bar, hence the name of the pub shed becoming, the Infinity Lounge. Good tips Dawn and Steven have for others looking to create a pub shed, are using left over wood to build your own bar, table and seating area. They also used a spare double glazed window which had shattered on one side, so they decided to recycle it and use it for the top of the bar.

THE *PUB SHEDS UK A-Z*

Jenabeck Lounge

Kevin Phillips, Maesteg

The main reason for the name, The Jenabeck Lounge, is that before we built the bar, the shed was originally being used as a dog kennel, for my wife's father to breed his dogs. His kennel club affix was Jenabeck (a combination of Jennifer-his wife- and Becky-his daughter) our bulldog Stan was also shown under the Jenabeck affix so it made sense to continue with the name. The theme for our pub shed was fairly obvious to us, as being from Wales we are both fanatical Welsh Rugby supporters; supporting both the national team and my local club Pontypridd RFC. Being a supporter of Pontypridd since I was a very young boy, I had amassed a lot of memorabilia, which I now have on display, including t-shirts, programs, tickets, flags and photos of players both past and present. All of the work done on the pub shed was carried out by myself and my wife Becky, and a lot of the items within the pub shed were from car bot sales, and various auction sites. I must say it has been a pleasure to build and design my very own pub shed, although it is something that will never be complete, as there are always things to add and things to change, such as different layouts. The pub shed has now become a part of life, as I am always thinking about what to do next. We are now in the second phase of the build as initially we didn't have a level floor; so, we had to fit a false floor. We also had a single skin tin roof which wasn't lined, leading to all sorts of condensation problems. A simple false ceiling and insulation overcame these issues. The floor was something that had to be corrected as it wasn't level and tables and chairs were also uneven, and after a few drinks people began falling over; the floor is now level, but somehow people still seem to fall over. Due to these changes the ceiling was also lowered, which means that anyone over 6ft is banned from the pub. The pub is a single skin breeze block, with a metal roof, and it stands at around 12 x 10 foot in size.

The Jockey

Ian Gibson, Rainford St. Helens

Having been a fan of the early series of Shameless, and having watched the cast gather together in their local, I decided to call my pub shed The Jockey as this was also the name used for the pub in the show. I also called it The Jockey as when we all get together in the pub shed it feels like all the riff raff just the same as on shameless. It was always my intention to build a pub shed, and when I eventually had my garden done, I made sure that there was enough space to install a base that would be big enough for a 14 x 10 foot pub shed. However, after having my shed installed at this size, the year after I increased it causing it to grow ever bigger. The Jockey now sits nicely in the corner of my garden in Rainford, St. Helens.

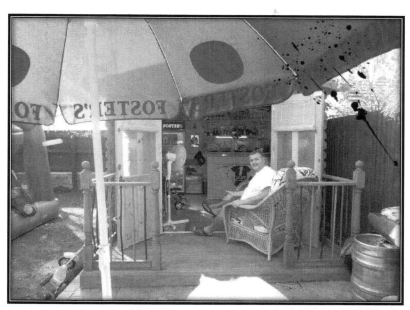

John & Nina's

John Willmott, Derby

I built my pub shed alongside my wife. We built the pub shed as we wanted an old style bar where we would be able to entertain friends and family. The main reason for naming our pub shed John and Nina's is that we did it all on our own, using our spare time to put everything together. Our pub shed measures 18 x 10 feet and it was constructed in the summer of 2013

Jackie's Bar

Jackie & Dave Allsop, Sutton-in-Ashfield,

Jackie's Bar was originally used as a weightlifting and games room for my husband Dave. It was one year ago when we went on holiday to Torquay, that the hotel we stayed in had a games room with pool and snooker tables etc. Dave and I often played pool, and we soon decided to buy a pool table of our own, and we placed it in our garage. This was when Dave decided to get rid of his weights, and we had the idea of turning it into our pub. Dave works 48 hours each week on continental shifts. When he used to come home he made a start on the work involved in transforming the garage, and sometimes he would stay in there until midnight, as he did all the work single handed. I would often help him with the cleaning up so that he could manoeuvre his way around. Twelve months later it is now finished, and we both decided that our pub should be named Jackie's Bar. Our bar is located in Sutton-in-Ashfield.

THE PUB SHEDS UK A-Z

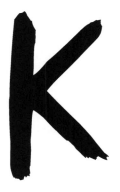

The Koi & Bulldog

Roy & Jenny Foster, Kirkby

Roy and Jenny Foster are the owners of The Koi and Bulldog pub shed. Their pub shed is located in Kirkby near Liverpool, and they have made sure that it is continually stocked with their own homebrewed ales, ciders and wines. The Koi and Bulldog was named after their pet bulldog and also after their pond full of Koi which sits next to their bar. Their pub shed was built in the summer of 2014 by Roy and his son jack (aged 15). It was built as they wanted a meeting place for the family, as Roy's mom had lung cancer for a 2nd time and she couldn't get out much. She now loves the bar and is still fighting the big C. Roy and Jenny joined Pub Sheds UK in 2015, and since then their bar has been transformed, with the great ideas from the group, giving them inspiration for pumps, music systems and lighting, as well as much more. The pub shed is now a complete addiction for the owners, and they often find themselves hunting through car bot sales in the search for more bar stuff.

The Kraken

Wayne Godfrey, Great Yarmouth

Welcome to The Kraken guys. This little pub shed started out its life as my dad's old garden shed. It was used as such for quite a few years and it had begun to see better days. Soon though however, I took it off his hands, and I decided to try and inject some life back into it. It was after seeing Pub Sheds UK that I decided that I wanted to convert it into a pub shed. I used a very low budget to complete the task, and to this day it is still a work in progress; nevertheless, I love it and it puts a smile on my face seeing my friends and family enjoying it. My pub shed is located in Hopton on sea, Great Yarmouth.

The Kennel

Samuel England, North Lincolnshire

Following the closure of the only pub in our village in 2013, the idea of having our own Pub Shed was planted. After several years of collecting random pieces of pub memorabilia and many boozy nights planning the perfect retreat... The Kennel was created. Due to a love of beer, darts, dominoes, dogs and all the fine qualities of a traditional British pub, we wasted no time in getting started on construction. We opened our pub shed in the summer of 2015. The Kennel is only 8 x 8 feet in size which is really quite modest when compared to some pub sheds, yet we feel that small is beautiful. Inside our pub shed there is one working hand pull, a Guinness surger unit and a Stella Artois font, which is used for ornamental purposes only. Our pub shed comfortably seats six people plus our three bulldogs. There are also plenty of extra seats and parasols in the garden, and also a genuine Kennel for our dogs. Anyone and everyone are welcome in our pub shed, and we regularly host ad-hoc parties for our friends and neighbours, which include the occasional darts and dominoes tournaments.

Kenty's

Mark & Sarah Kent, Leicestershire

Kenty's is a recently built pub shed located in Leicestershire. It's a 12 x 10 foot summerhouse which took me around three months to decide upon. I chose the shed as I wanted to go with a more modern looking pub, and seeing as it had a lot of windows, it was perfect for achieving that bright and modern look. Size wise, it is also perfect for all I wanted to include in my pub. I have managed to get enough seating for twelve people inside; it also has a bar area with fully functional taps and optics and more importantly it also has a dartboard. Naming the pub shed was really quite simple, as "Kenty's" is just a slight extension of my surname, and it is also what my friends and family know me as. To all those people reading this, if you are contemplating building your own pub shed… then go for it, as it's the best thing I have ever done. Just do your homework, and make sure you know what style you want before you build one.

THE **PUB SHEDS UK** A-Z

Little Brockville

James Mcarthur, Falkirk

My pub shed is called Little Brockville, and it is located in Falkirk in central Scotland. It was named after the Falkirk football clubs old ground, which was where I watched my local team as a young lad. My pub shed started its life as a workshop for one of my friends; it was this same friend that was also the person who built the shed. However, soon after building the shed it was decided that it wasn't going to be big enough for a workshop, so I ended up adopting it, and from that moment my pub shed was born. I can honestly say that building my bar has become a project, and one that I hold most highly; it is also a project that I feel I will never finish, as there is just so much you can do, and so many things you can change and add; it is sort of my "creative obsession" I think this term best describes what it is like to own your own pub shed.

125

Luke's Bar

Mark & Elaine Farmer, West Yorkshire

Luke's Bar was made in honour of my son, and rifleman, Luke Farmer of the 3 Rifles, who was killed in action in Afghanistan 2010. Our pub shed is used regularly by friends and family, and we have had some good times in the bar, always raising a glass to our hero. Myself and Mark Farmer - the landlord and also the father of Luke - thought that building a tribute to Luke was a great idea, because he would have loved it. We have had many great time in Luke's Bar and there will be many more in the years to come. Our pub shed is situated in a little village called Upton in West Yorkshire.

Le Bar Anglaise

Tony McCawley, Brackley

Le Bar Anglaise all started when I visited my father's house in France. The house was a traditional French property where they had been working on renovation for many years. There was also a swimming pool in the garden, yet it was too far from the house... and the fridge. A simple bar was then devised to make it easier to reach and it was called 'Le Bar'. In November 2012 I moved house, and the new house had a larger garden. With this extra space I was able to reconstruct a new shed in the summer of 2013, and I transformed it into a bar. The naming of my pub shed was simply 'Le Bar Anglaise'. Much of the internal construction was comprised of pallets, with the bar worktop having been made from a left over kitchen renovation. The shed is fully insulated with polystyrene boxes and packing material and all the furniture was purchased second hand, including the two beautiful leather chairs. During the summer of 2014 I saw a 6 x 7 foot shed in need of a new home, so I used it to extend my own shed. The end of the bar was removed and I began work on adding the extension. Ultimately 2 metres was added to my original shed. I also added batons to the new roof, and I insulated the walls with plaster board from a builder's yard; I also managed to find a log burner at a low price which I placed in the newly built lounge area. The base of the shed is bricks and the hearth is a large paving slab.

The Lochar Cocker Inn

Richard Jahn, Dumfries

The Lochar Cocker Inn is owned by Richard Jahn, and it was opened on Boxing Day 2014. The name of the pub shed comes from the Lochar River which runs close to the village, and it pays tribute to Ralph, a true pub dog with a love for real ale. The pub shed serves a wide range of drinks from working hand pumps and the favoured ale is provided by a local microbrewery - Andrews Ales - which is just ten minutes down the road. Richard decided that he needed his own pub shed after visiting a friends back garden hostelry and seeing the many benefits it provided. He enjoys old fashioned pubs and real ale, so the chance to combine the two and have them on his own doorstep was too good to miss. His partner took a bit more convincing, but finally came around to the idea... that was, after a promise of lots of gin and tonic, and no more messy parties in the house. The option to expand and build a pool room is still up for debate. The pub shed was built over a period of six months with the help from neighbours, friends and family, who were always on the hunt for items to decorate the shed. Richards theme of ' up-cycling' has seen him become inventive with odd acquisitions such as an RAC sign turned into a table, a bar rail made from some left over disabled handrail and an antler coat hook, (because everyone has a friend who makes antler chandeliers don't they?) A good tip for other budding pub shed builders would be that if you don't ask, you don't get; having a carpet fitted in the spare room led to a lovely pure wool tartan carpet for the pub when Richard spotted the offcut at the back of the carpet showroom. Another good piece of advice which comes in handy is from Richards's dad, *"Accept all but blows!"*

THE PUB SHEDS UK A-Z

The Mount Nod

Mick Friar, Coventry

The Mount Nod pub shed was born after watching "Shed of the Year", it was after seeing the pub category that I thought, "I could build one of them!" as I'm the kind of person who always needs to be involved in a project. The first phase of The Mount Nod was an 8 x 8 foot shed, which I picked up off eBay; however, as I am a handyman, whose skills were passed down from my late father, I hand built everything internally including the bar, the back bar and pretty much everything else. The theme was always to try and make it look old; like the kind of pub that your parents frequented, not like the soulless pubs you see today. eBay was the main place that I obtained the kind of internal touches that I wanted, however it proved quite expensive, so that's when I discovered car boot sales. We have had many fantastic buys from these, picking things up for as little as 20 pence. The only problem with building a pub in your back garden is that you attract a lot of friends; ones that you didn't know you had; this of course, led to an extension of another 10 x 8 feet. This extension provided more seating and a big screen projector for all those important football games. However, this didn't come without problems; I had built at an angle to follow the fence line and the roof was a b*st*rd to get right. The reason for the name of the pub shed is really quite simple; it's because we live in the Mount Nod area of Coventry, so it felt appropriate, and "Mick and Jo's" or "MJ's" all sounded quite modern. My top tip is: build as big as the space you have available allows, or you will find yourself having to extend in no time; also, choose your friends wisely and check out your local car boot sales for the best bargains.

Mona's Bar

David & Simone Massam, St. Helens Merseyside

Monas Bar was named after me, as it was a nickname given to me by my late Nan; she used to call me 'Monie'. The main structure of the bar was built from recycled wood, and the main purpose for it having been built was so that we could enjoy a beer, and have a dance in a nice family friendly environment. These reasons are exactly why our pub shed is used, and we spend a lot of quality time together with family and friends. Inside the pub shed we have a 42" TV with Sky TV attached, we also have a boom box so that we can play our music, and alongside this it also has three refrigerators, and Fosters and John Smiths on draught. Our pub shed is also open all year round!

The Monkey Bar

Conor Keatings, Ireland

The Monkey Bar is located in Ireland, and it is probably the smallest pub you will be able to find there. This pub shed has a proper bar, a regulation size dart board, vintage signs and bar stools. As well as these additions it also has a comfy leather recliner which is the perfect spot to sit and watch sports events. The shed is quite standard but it has been decorated in the style of a Shebeen bar, and a carpenter friend of the owner built the bar by hand. The owner has also picked up many bargains online and from salvage yards, as well as car bot sales in an attempt to decorate his pub shed. The monkey bar is the perfect little place to hang out with friends.

Molly's Bar

Rich Ellerington, Hull

My bar is called Molly's Bar; we chose this particular name, as when we were building it, we unfortunately lost our dog, whose name was also Molly. The shed is 10 x 8 foot in size, and we decided to build it due to their not being enough space when the time came for having parties with family and friends. The bar itself is made of pieces of old wood, and a pack of flooring that was on offer at the time at a DIY store. It was our local pub that helped us with the decorations for the interior of our pub shed; they kindly provided us with old items that they no longer had any use for. Our pub shed is located in Hull.

THE PUB SHEDS UK A-Z

The Not Out Inn

Steve Hall & Andrea Dicks, Wigan

The Not Out Inn was based on a conversation that I had with my partner, Andrea. The conversation was about the days when we used to go out every weekend, seeing the same faces, and always in the same place, and we had begun feeling that it didn't quite have the appeal that it used to. So in order to try and relive our youth - without having to wait around for taxis - we decided that we would have it all conveniently placed in our own back yard; this way we would be able to have our friends come to us. Since then our pub shed has been a roaring success, and we have had many good nights in The Not Out Inn. Our pub shed is located in Wigan, and it is 6 x 4 feet in size.

The Nobody Inn

Valetia & Jim Dunham, Norwich

The Nobody Inn started being constructed in June 2014, and it was later completed in March 2015. The pub shed was built by my husband Jim, my brother Kevin and a friend of Jim's called Tony. The size of our pub shed is 13 x 14 foot and it was built entirely from scratch. It also has an arbour attached onto it, so as to provide a convenient space for outdoor seating. Our pub shed is located in Norwich, Norfolk.

The Nags Head

Jason & Wendy Speedy, Newcastle-Under-Lyme

The Nags Head pub shed is owned by Jason and Wendy Speedy and it is located in Newcastle-Under-Lyme, Staffordshire. The Nags Head started out its life as an 8 x 6 foot summerhouse, back in 2011. Eventually the summerhouse was kitted out and turned it into a pub shed. Soon it became a firm favourite among their friends and family, and it became a great place for them to host parties. They also often use their pub shed to watch the football with the lads. In 2012 they also added another 8 x 8 foot summerhouse onto the existing one so that they could have a lounge and sizable seating area.

The Naggs Shed

Toby McCartney, Eaglesfield

My wife and I used to go to a comedy night on a Friday, when we used to live in London; it was usually hosted in a pub called The Naggs Head on the Finchley road. So, when it came to us having our own pub shed it only seemed right to call it The Naggs Shed. The Naggs Shed is also on Google maps, and it is located in a small village called Eaglesfield near to Lockerbie Dumfriesshire. In our pub shed we have beer on tap, Guinness and any spirit you can imagine. Alongside the drinks we also have a jukebox, fruit machine, dart board and of course, free drink, which all makes for quite awesome parties. Each New Year we also have a fancy dress party and there are usually around twenty five people who come to enjoy the night. The Naggs Shed was established in 2013, as my wife wasn't happy with me because our shed was sitting full of stuff that wasn't being used; so, I decided to clear the shed out and I took a lot of the items to a car boot sale, whereby I was able to make a few hundred pounds. Due to this I now saw that my shed had quite a lot of free space, so then the idea for turning it into a pub shed hit me. I spent the money I had earnt from the car boot and I created The Naggs Shed. Three of my friends now also have their own pub shed… so let the legacy continue.

THE **PUB SHEDS** UK A-Z

The Outside Inn

Trevor Hewer, Western Lake District

The Outside Inn pub shed is located in the Western Lake District, Cumbria. The idea for our pub shed was provided by my wife, as she was the one who originally showed me a picture of one on Facebook, which caused me to instantly fall in love with the idea. I worked on the idea of having one of my own for around one month; until finally it arrived from a shed building company. For the shed and the quality that I required, it was cheaper to buy one from a shed merchant. Since then I have dedicated my heart and soul to it as well as some of my skills as a joiner. The pub shed is 14 x 6 foot in size and I named it The Outside Inn, predominantly because of the fact that when you're out... you're also in. My pub shed was born on 3rd May 2015 and I love it. The biggest project I would like to do, is dig out a cellar... Maybe one day this will happen.

156

O'Smithers

Doug Smith, Hambleton

The O'Smithers pub shed was built in 2014 by me and my good friend, Billy Mitchell. Overall it took around three months to build and I have been adding to it ever since. It is a wooden shed that has got three large shutters, so that it can be entirely enclosed or open on three sides when the weather permits. O'Smithers is an Irish Rugby themed bar and it is 12 x 22 foot in size. Most of the bar accessories were sourced through eBay, with the biggest bargain being the projector TV that I picked up for just £0.99 pence. As well as this the pub shed has a 50 inch TV, Sonas music system/jukebox, Wi-Fi, ice machine, glass washer, triple bar fridge, seven optics, a wine chiller, karaoke machine, bar bell, tea/coffee machine, a bingo machine and four draught beers including Guinness. The pub shed was called O'Smithers because I originate from Southern Ireland, and my name is Smith. The Irish Rugby theme comes because I am Irish and I love rugby. The pub shed was also built in memory of my late dad, who always enjoyed a good drink. As you approach the front of the building it has all the appearances of a bar, but from the rear, it looks like you are looking at the Blackpool tower building, with a 24 foot replica of Blackpool tower on the roof of the pub. My tower was built in 1940 by apprentices from Vickers Armstrong, who made the Wellington Bomber during the 2nd world war at Blackpool airport. It was rediscovered down in Cornwall in a very poor state. When it was brought back to Lancashire, I had it totally restored, including illuminations, and it is now situated on top of the pub shed, and can be admired by many. I feel that my pub shed is a great place to spend time with good friends, exchanging stories and having a drink or two. The craic is always mighty!!! The pub shed is located in Hambleton which is eight miles out from Blackpool, so from my bath you can see not one, but two Blackpool towers.

The Olive Tree

Lynn & Brian Hughes, St. Helens Merseyside

The Olive Tree is located in St. Helens, Merseyside and it is owned by Lynn and Brian Hughes. My pub shed is 12 x 10 feet in size, and it was named after my mother in law, whose name was also Olive; she sadly passed away. The pub shed was also named after a tree that we have in our garden. The Olive Tree is great for all our family and friends to come and entertain, and it is also regularly used as a place for watching sports.

The Original Tattooed Arms

Dave.T.Taylor, Bolton

The Original Tattooed Arms was built in 2010 by me and some of my close friends. We decided to build our own bar at the bottom of my back garden, predominantly due to the frustration caused by the hiking beer prices and the smoking ban, as well as the fact that our local pub didn't have a TV available for us to watch the 2010 World Cup. We named our pub shed The Tattooed Arms because I am a tattoo artist and many of my friends have tattooed arms. It was in 2015 that we found out that there was another pub shed with this same name, so we decided to change it to The Original Tattooed Arms.

162

THE *PUB SHEDS UK* A-Z

The Priory

Gary Jackson, South Elmsall West Yorkshire

The Priory pub shed has been made from two plastic sheds joined together to make one 8 x 16 foot shed. My pub shed is located in South Elmsall in West Yorkshire, and it was named for two reasons. The first reason is that I live on the Priory estate, and the second reason is that I thought it would be a good twist, by using the same name as a famous London clinic known for helping alcoholics. We also have a cocktail at The Priory called Rehab too. The Priory pub shed is fully insulated and it even has its own electrics and retro light bulbs. When creating my pub shed I went for an oldie worldie pub style as this is where I find myself most at home when I'm out. My pub shed is made from mostly dark wood and brass fittings like elephant handrails, pressure gauge clock and brass trip trays, all of which adds to the decorative theme. The inside is also carpeted throughout, and recently the seating has changed from an old church pew into a more comfortable leather couch. There is also a pub table made by hand in Scotland from solid oak along with traditional pub stools. The Flying Scotsman Plaque I have in the pub is there as a way of remembering my grandad who was a boiler man on the same train during its world record speed run. I have tried to keep the interior theme oak dark wood and brass with vintage fittings like coat hooks from salvage yards. There is also a brick effect wallpaper and wood effect wallpaper which made the project cheaper and easier to achieve. The pub shed also has a main bar complete with pumps and back bar with bottle display stands and a Priory mirror. We use our pub shed all the time and are looking forward to trying out our first winter in it, which shouldn't be a problem now that it is insulated and I have installed a heating system using slim panel heaters on the walls.

Family and friends use it on the weekends, and for birthdays etc. but the best for us is when me and the missus go in for no reason for a few drinks and a chat as well as a bit of TV as we also have Sky TV installed and a Bose sound system for music. I have ongoing plans at the minute for a jukebox to be built, and one thing a pub shed should never be without is bacon fries; I feel it is not a proper pub shed without them. I also had a lot of help from fellow Pub Sheds UK member Chris Cowley, the landlord of Samples Cider Bar

Priory Taps

Mark Ted Edwards, Kingston Upon Hull

Our pub shed was named The Priory Taps because we live on Priory road and we also have Foster's lager and Strongbow dark fruits on tap, so the reasons behind our name were pretty straight forward. We wanted to create our pub shed and use it as a sports bar, as we are Hull City and Hull FC fans, so we wanted to carry the theme of this into our bar. We have also recently transformed our beer garden, so now the bar has regular locals, who often come around for a quiet night...at least, that's how they start, until one of our friends ends up coming around the next morning apologising for the night before! So we now tell people before they get too drunk what flowers we want the next day.

The Pallet Bar

David Nix, Dorset

For a long time I had dreamt of owning my very own man cave/bar. I wanted it to be somewhere I could go to watch F1 in peace and do "man" things. We originally bought a 3 x 3 metre summer house so that we could use it as an office space for my wife; however, due to a change in career it was no longer required. What a result for me! Finally I had a room that I could call my own; however, as cash flow wasn't great, I decided to build my bar out of reclaimed pallets, which I dismantled and re-cut, before then sanding them and staining the wood. As time has moved by friends and family have donated many items to me and I have also used eBay and car boot sales, which have all helped me find bits and pieces to decorate my pub shed. I found a fridge on eBay which cost just £21 and I cut it to fit in the bar. In total my pub shed has cost me just £50 so far, and although it isn't yet quite finished it should be fully open in around two weeks. As the bar was mainly constructed using pallets, it seemed to me that the only logical name for my new man cave would be The Pallet Bar.

170

The Poachers Rest

Ian & Jill Humphreys, Somercotes Derbyshire

Hi, this is Ian and Jill Humphreys and we run The Poachers Rest in Somercotes, Derbyshire. Our pub shed is dedicated to my late father in law, as we have a few items that he used to have in his own bar. As a keen shooter and the occasional poaching excursion back in my youth, it was the obvious choice to name our pub shed The Poachers Rest. We have styled our pub on a traditional old fashioned pub which focuses on shooting and fishing memorabilia, most of which was sourced from our local car boot sales. We have had many drunken nights with friends and family and also on occasion with just the two of us. We had our pub shed made by a local company but all the interior work was completed by myself, under the watchful eye of the Mrs. The best comment we have received was from a close friend who said *"If all pubs were like this, I would start going out again!"* this made all the hard work worth wile, and we love our pub.

THE PUB SHEDS UK A-Z

THE OFFICIAL GUIDE 2015

Pub Sheds UK

Quiz

In order to try and break up the book and provide you with some momentary enjoyment, we thought we would add in this little quiz. The quiz also comprises of some questions relating to this very book (so let's see if you have been paying attention) you can either take the quiz now or leave it until you have finished the book; because the questions relate to the entire book, and not just to what you have read already… enjoy!

1. Crystal clear beer is an indication of what?
   A)   Too much light during the malting.
   B)   Too much water was absorbed into the grain during the milling process.
   C)   Neither of these answers.

2. How is beer ranked in the world's most popular drinks?
   A) Worlds 1st most popular
   B) Worlds 2nd most popular
   C) Worlds 3rd most popular

3. Which US state is labelled on a Jack Daniels bottle?

A)   Tennessee

B)   Memphis

C)   California

4. What is the average number of grapes needed to produce a bottle of wine?

A)   1000

B)   600

C)   1600

5. When was beer first sold in cans?

A)   1925

B)   1930

C)   1935

6. What is the literal translation of Vodka?

A)   Big water

B)   Little water

C)   Medium water

THE *PUB SHEDS UK* A-Z

7. Why is there an indentation at the bottom of wine bottles?
   A)   To strengthen the bottle
   B)   To aid in holding the bottle
   C)   Merely for decoration

8. What is added to a drink when ordered neat?
   A)   Water
   B)   Crushed ice
   C)   Nothing

9. What alcoholic beverage is Homer Simpson's drink of choice?
   A)   Bloody caeser
   B)   Duff beer
   C)   Manhattan

10. Which Pub Shed in this A-Z has won Pub Shed of the year twice?
   A)   The Mount Nod
   B)   3 Steps Bar
   C)   The Wheel Inn

11. Where was the replica Blackpool Tower
from O'Smithers pub shed rediscovered?
A) Great Yarmouth
B) Torquay
C) Cornwall

12. From what TV Series did The Jockey
pub shed get the idea for its name?
A) Shameless
B) Only Fools and Horses
C) Two Pints of Lager and a Packet of Crisps

13. What was the Jenabeck Lounge pub shed
originally used for?
A) Dog Kennel
B) Rabbit House
C) Chicken Shed

14. Where in the West Midlands is Georges Bar
pub shed Located?
A) Wolverhampton
B) Birmingham
C) Walsall

15. What charity was the UK Flag Challenge
created for?
A) Tunza's Pride
B) British Heart Foundation
C) Children in Need

Answers:

A :15 ;A :14 ;A :13 ;A :12
C :11 ;B :10 ;B :9 ;A :8 ;B :7 ;C :6 ;B :5 ;A :4 ;B :3 ;B :2
!up you sober and try to water
you giving are people means it clear is it If (C) :1

THE OFFICIAL GUIDE 2015

THE *PUB SHEDS UK* A-Z

The Rock Shed

Graham Kinked, Newtownabbey

My name is Graham Kinked from Newtownabbey, Co Antrim, Northern Ireland and I am the owner of The Rock Shed. The idea for my pub shed came from me getting hassle from my wife Pamela, for always playing rock music in the house; so, that's when I decided to take it outside to the shed. I then turned my work shed into a rock shed, and my friends and family now love it. We love having rock nights in with mates and my family and we also have many other get togethers. My pub shed has two refrigerators, a heater, TV, DVD player and a record player. It is also open all year round.

Ramshack

Glenn Parkes, Bilsthorpe Nottinghamshire

The Ramshack pub shed has been created from sourcing many free materials, and we have really come to like to the look of it. The theme of the Ramshack wasn't planned either, as it has gradually evolved with what we have been able to source. As time has gone by however, it has begun to take on the look of an old English pub, and it continues to do so. The name of the Ramshack came about because of the radio station that we often help out with from time to time, and also a station that we would spend hours listening to. Our pub shed is 30 x 22 foot in size with an extension and it can be found in Bilsthorpe, Nottinghamshire.

𝕽other's 𝕽eturn

Shane Rothery, Barrow in Furness

My pub shed is located in Barrow in Furness, and it was built by me and college apprentices, who needed the work experience in construction. The pub shed comprises of block built walls and smooth render. The inspiration for building the shed came about due to a bet made by one of my friends who said, *"You'll never build it!"* so I proved him wrong. I now want to extend a veranda onto the beer garden with a flag pole and outdoor heating and lighting. The name of the Rother's Return is an improvisation mixing both elements of my name and the Rovers Return.

The Royal Damper

Lorraine & Terry Nicolas, Warrington Cheshire

The Royal Damper is located in Warrington, Cheshire. The name for this pub shed came about because we used to have a campervan which we called the 'Damper' as we would have a 'damp' (drink) in a friends pub and then stumble back to the *'Dampervan'*; the royal part was added as we both have Highland Lord and Lady titles.

THE *PUB SHEDS UK A-Z*

S

The Shed Bit

Adam Simmons, Norwich Norfolk

My shed came to be around 1998, and originally it started out its life as one beer barrel and some of my home brew. Over the years it has just grown and grown, and at my place of work it has become an institution to visit. For the last thirteen years the same group of friends have met in the shed to celebrate national Milligan day, which is a fictional bank holiday. I named my pub shed, The Shed Bit because that's what it was before I set about changing it, by getting rid of the lawn mowers and tools and replacing them with a bar and beer. A great tip that I feel I should share with other sheddies is: make it your own, and make it the way you want it. My pub shed is located in Norwich, Norfolk.

Shannon's Bar

Ian Mackinnon, Grangemouth Scotland

Shannon's Bar was named after our daughter Shannon who sadly passed away ten years ago aged 8. It is not so much the bar itself, but rather the whole garden that acts as a small memorial to her; it is also a beer garden that is used by family and friends. The bar is themed around a small rum shack, and it is based on ideas we have taken from beach bars that we often visit whilst we are in Ibiza; the surrounding garden also has the same theme. Everything we have created has been dressed with bamboo and palm trees, all of which adds to the exotic feel that we were looking for. The pub shed also features an outside seating area which has its own roof. I also built everything myself, using the cash that I had inherited from my grandad who loved a good old fashioned get together, and a drink; so he would have been chuffed with the outcome of the bar. Altogether I have used 33 wooden pallets to build the bar. So in a nutshell, Shannon's Bar is a tribute to everything that means a lot to us, from family past and present and also family holidays. In the future we hope to continue building upon the character of the shed, and hopefully we will use it often with family and friends. Our pub shed is located in a town called Grangemouth in-between Glasgow and Edinburgh, Scotland.

Steel Horse Saloon

Damian Lord Wass, Chesterfield

I built my Steel Horse Saloon pub shed, as I wanted somewhere that I could store my Harley's. My girlfriend had already got a concreate base down, so she said it would be ok to put something on it. I then got to work building the shed myself, and it took me just two days to construct it using log lap timber; using this made the pub shed look more like a Wild West Saloon. Originally I had one Harley in the shed for about a week, before I then got to work building a makeshift bar. Soon I also added a log burner, and then out went the old bar, and in went a new one. I then began filling the pub shed with many pub related items including a real jukebox. I have now been kicked out of the house as far as brewing goes so it is now all done in my saloon. We spend many hours in our pub shed, and we have had a few friends come around and they absolutely love it. As for the name "Steel Horse Saloon" that is what the Americans used to call Harley's when they first came out.

Shenanigans Irish Bar

Darren & Michelle Phelps, South Wales

The outside of our pub shed comes complete with home-made window shutters which were made from pallets, and on the door we have also advertised the opening hours of 10am-4am. Inside our pub shed we wanted to aim for the oldy worldy feel, and this again was created using pallets for panelling before then adding dark wood varnish. The furniture also matches and it was finished off with a log store alcove. We chose the Irish theme for our pub shed down to our love of old Irish pubs, due to us having stayed in Ireland on a few Rugby weekends, so that we could watch Wales play Ireland. It was during those times that we fell in love with Irish culture and music. The name Shenanigans was down to my wife, who was the one who gave me the idea, as on weekends she would say *"do you want to go up the shed for some drunken shenanigans?"* (nothing rude intended may I add). The shed (which is an old garage) was divided into two sections three years ago, as it wasn't being used for anything else. The front section was used as playroom for the children; however, due to the children using it very little I decided to convert it into a pub. In the beginning it was just a bar and a settee. Since being built we have had friends contacting us asking how they get to Shenanigans because it's not on Google maps, as they began thinking a new pub had opened in the area. My intentions for the future are to convert the second section of the garage into a pool room, which will also have fruit machines. My favourite quotes are *"You can't drink all day if you don't start in the morning"* and *"We only drink because no great story started with someone eating a salad"* and some tips I would share with others sheddies are; don't break your bank account, use charity shops and car boot sales, and make good use of pallets to get an oldy worldy look. Shenanigans can be found in Maesteg in South Wales.

199

THE PUB SHEDS UK A-Z

Tiki Bar

Kevin Pearson, Wakefield, West Yorkshire

This is my Tiki Bar, which was named by my wife, (not sure why she would name it Tiki Bar). Our pub shed is located in Wakefield in West Yorkshire, and it was first built to house all the rubbish which had been taken out of our garage in order to get the car in. However, when it was finished, my wife decided to turn it into a bar instead (that was two years ago) and in the last sixth months we have just finished adding a 6 x 8 foot extension and we have also refurbished the bar, so our pub shed is now 18 x 6 foot in size and the refurbishment only cost around £150. 90% of the build didn't cost anything, as I managed to get all the timber from work, as they were throwing it away. I also got the windows from a skip behind a replacement window manufacturer, and the paving slabs were from Grimsby fish docks. The bar top came from a caravan manufacturer in Hull. The only cost for the pub shed was the roofing felt, along with the nails, locks and hinges etc. Over the last two years we have been able to have some great party's in our pub shed, and we have also done a Christmas tribute to live aid, and we had a great laugh and lots of fun. Two weeks after this we had a live aid party to celebrate its 30 years. In total it took around 6 months to build our pub shed, along with the help of my best mate Andy Croft; we built our pub shed in all conditions including wind, rain, sun and snow. Nevertheless, the entertainment we have all had from our pub shed made all that hard work more than worth it.

The Three Hairs
Lee Tattam, Chippenham

After the birth of my first born a couple of years ago, my dad advised me that I needed a shed; so, on dad's advice The Three Hairs was born. It probably wasn't quite what he had in mind, but I don't like gardening... I like beer! I thought of many names for my pub shed - most of which id be too embarrassed to repeat to family members-, so I opted for The Three Hairs in reference to the lack of hair on my head. Originally I intended for my pub shed to be a sports bar, but after buying a number of retro pub memorabilia pieces at car boot sales it has evolved into a 'Traditional English Pub'. My next step in the future is to get Sky TV and also begin making my own real ales. My pub shed is 10 x 8 foot in size and it is located in Colerne, Chippenham. A picture of The Three Hairs has also been used on a well-known dating site by my sister as her profile picture, and she now gets more questions about the pub shed than about her; she says the pub shed has ruined her life (whilst she necks a gin and tonic!)

Tizzers Tavern

Paul Tyrrell, Rochdale

My name is Paul Tyrrell, and my nickname is Tizzer. In 2010 whilst I was serving in the British Army in Germany, I opened Tizzers Tavern in my basement of my Married Quarter. The reasons behind this is that during the drawdown of the forces leaving Germany, most of the amenities and bars in and around the barracks were closing, so about forty of us decided to make our own bars, and do our own pub crawls at the weekend. The first Tizzers Tavern was located at the Bruggen Barracks in Germany. When I left the forces in 2012, I decided to keep the tradition going and I wanted to theme it on looking like a Warrant Officers and Sgt's Mess Bar. As I was limited for space in my garden, I decided to convert my garage, as it was only being used to hoard old military photos and some football memorabilia. The early stages of the conversion began in 2013, and to date it has been the focus of my favourite hobby… drinking, and I'm always trying to improve its looks by adding extra things to it each month. The majority of the lads that converted their own basements have now also come back to the UK, and they have carried on the tradition which makes our pub crawling officially national.

The Tipsy Bar

Daren Williams, Welsh Valleys Ebbw Vale

My name is Daren Williams and here is my pub shed, also known as The Tipsy Bar. My pub shed is located in the Welsh valleys, Ebbw Vale, South Wales. I came up with the name Tipsy Bar after the concrete base was laid under the influence of a vast amount of Stella, so the floor ended up becoming a little tipsy. From day one ¾ of the neighbourhood all came together at The Tipsy Bar, and we are currently in talks with the female members to add an extra room, which will be outfitted with a hot tub and a sauna… so watch this space.

Tels Tavern

Terry Wadman, London

My name is Terry Wadman, and I'm the landlord of Tels Tavern. I decided to build my pub shed to coincide with the 2014 World Cup. My son also urged me to build it after he saw a similar one in a friend's garden. The naming of my shed is self-explanatory, as my name is Tel so a friend suggested Tels Tavern. I already had a shed on site and thought I would extend it to begin with; however, once I started it became obvious that it needed a complete rebuild. So I decided on a 10 x 12 foot shed, and I purchased 5 x 2 treated timber for the base and sat it on concrete blocks, then I constructed the walls from 3x2 and OSB boards. The shed cost me around £2000 to build and I kitted it out with pub equipment from eBay and car boot sales, and the bar counter is an old kitchen work top I had off a friend. I completed my pub shed in May 2014 in time for England's opening game of the 2014 World Cup against Italy. I had 19 people inside the shed, and it was well and truly tested when England scored, as the place erupted and the shed remained intact, so I knew I had done a good job. I now use my shed regularly for family gatherings and parties, and I would urge anyone with the time, space, and of course, the money, to build one as I am so glad that I did.

THE PUB SHEDS UK A-Z

UK FLAG CHALLENGE

A note from Mike Bacon:

The flag challenge was an idea that I had in order to try and bring the group together and to also get members involved in something that is worthwhile. The flag travelled around the country to different pub sheds so that the landlord or landlady could have a photo taken with the flag before signing it with their pub shed name/town/city and then post it to the next person. At the end of the flag challenge the flag had been to around 40 pub sheds by the end of August 2015. Now that the challenge is finished the flag will be auctioned off on the Pub Sheds UK group, hopefully in September or October; and all money raised will be donated to The Tunza Pride children's charity, which is based in St. Helens, Merseyside. The Tunza Pride charity has a centre that offer's children, young people and their families and everyone in the town a new place to spend time, learn new skills and socialise. They also run regular weekly activities as well as special events on weekends and school holiday periods - ranging from sports, music clubs, dance sessions, arts and crafts, singing classes, and alongside this they also have a café and a bar, which I help out with by keeping their beer lines clean, and I also help with events that they hold; so I felt that Pub Sheds UK could do its bit for an excellent charity and do Tunza's Pride proud. The flag used in the challenge is also the official banner used for the group.

About Tunza's Pride:

Tunza's Pride is a St Helens based charity which aims to help vulnerable children and young people in the Merseyside and North West region. They work hard to provide their own projects and also work in partnership with similarly minded organisations to develop joint activities. Since 2004, "Tunza" has successfully supported over 500 children and young people in a variety of ways and their vision is to help thousands more over the next few years. Backed by a team of Trustees dedicated to providing excellent projects with positive outcomes, "Tunza" is constantly looking at new ways of providing suitable activities for children and young people to participate in to help them achieve something amazing. Tunza Celebrity Supporters include Paul Wellens, Carley Stenson and Simon Rimmer – they have also worked with The Steven Gerrard Foundation to help change young people's lives.

THE *PUB SHEDS UK* A-Z

THE UK FLAG CHALLENGE

THE *PUB SHEDS UK* A-Z

𝖁𝖆𝖗𝖎𝖆𝖓𝖙 𝖕𝖚𝖇𝖘

When it comes to creating your own pub shed, not everyone is able to create a full shed. This could be due to having a lack of space when it comes to building one, or it could be due to them not having a big enough budget to buy a proper shed; but the main reason people don't have a full shed, is that they probably didn't want one… because great things can be achieved without even owning a shed. This section covers the variants; these are the pub sheds, which have been given a twist; they still have the usual pub related elements such as bar pulls, stools, and of course alcohol, but they differ from others because they are open, without sides or windows, and they have a more natural façade. These variant bars show you that you can have your own home pub without having to have a large space or shed.

The Retreat

Luke Staples, Nottingham

I have been waiting to get the bar for around four years, and I finally took the plunge to install it this year… and I really wish I had done it years ago. My bar has brought the family together and we have created so many memories. We also have our own Facebook page where we advertise events for all of our family and friends to see. We named our bar The Retreat when we moved into our new place and we began designing the garden; our plan was to create a place to retreat to at the bottom of the garden, including a bar and hot tub. The bar is 6 x 4 feet in size and we are looking to extend it and make an indoor section for those typical wet British days.

The Olive Tree

Antonia Jones, Burscough

The following pictures are of our Mediterranean outside bar called The Olive Tree. Our home bar was built by my husband Paul over a twelve month period. Having our home bar has made our garden much more enticing, and with the Mediterranean theme, we feel as though we are abroad every time we step outside.

229

𝕭𝖆𝖙𝖊𝖘 𝕭𝖆𝖗

Andy Bates

This is Bates Bar, and it is a bar that was made entirely from recycled wood and pallets. In total the entire bar including the fridge cost me around £45. Bates Bar was inspired by my daughter who said to me a couple of months ago, "Daddy, when we have our next BBQ party, you know what we need… a pub!" so as a dutiful father I built one. My daughter is only six, but both she and my son love serving behind the bar. In the future I hope to move onto creating a beer garden.

Lagoon Bar

Mally Davidson, Hull

Lagoon Bar is situated on a quiet street in Hull… it was quiet until the bar opened that is. The bar was named after our wedding location in Cyprus, and it was built and opened in 2013 to serve as a quality place to drink and eat with friends and family. We now host regular BBQ's and parties and the bar is often superbly decorated by my children and wife for theme nights, ranging from the World Cup to Halloween. Future projects on the horizon include, adding beer pumps, outdoor pizza oven and a jukebox. A trip to America this year will also provide us with many decorative items, such as glasses, beer mats, and license plates to attach to the front of the bar. If you are ever passing through the area, feel free to join us for a beer, cocktail or a shot of your choice.

Open all Hours Bar N Grill

Chris Hopwood,

This is my bar; the Open all Hours Bar N Grill. It has been built around nine weeks now, and I built it because I needed something adding to my garden; so, I got rid of the grass, and laid a patio, I then got to work creating my very own home bar.

Danny's Bar

Danny Wardale, Liverpool

My bar is called Danny's Bar and it is located in Liverpool. The entire bar was made from recycled materials and was built with my own two hands. The reason I had the bar was that my neighbour also has one, so I wanted to join in. There are now four bars all next door to each other, and we have a bar crawl every now and again. My neighbour is called John Kenny and he has a bar called Taffy's 2; his father passed away a couple of years ago, so he built his bar in his memory.

Parker's Bar

Sean Parker, Snaith

Parkers Bar was built in 2015 and it only took one weekend to finish. The bar cost around £200, and it has a built in BBQ. It is especially great for parties, as it has a 1600 watt sound system. I created the bar for some outdoor fun and didn't have enough room to have a full sized shed.

THE OFFICIAL GUIDE 2015

THE PUB SHEDS UK A-Z

The Woodworm Inn

Lee Emmerson, Gateshead

The Woodworm Inn probably spent about ten years in my head as a mere idea before I actually got around to starting the building of it. Over the years I have bought lots of bits and pieces and I have amassed quite a collection of glasses, bar runners and other breweriana, most of which I have picked up from eBay. When I started to build my pub shed I didn't really have a plan; I instead had a pile of wood, some screws and a rough idea. The name for my pub shed came from my mate, who initially looked at the bar and said "I've got one word for you… woodworm!" hence the name becoming The Woodworm Inn. My pub she has got Stella on draught and a fridge for other drinks, so it is a great way to spend warm summer nights (when we get them). The Woodworms twitter page (woodworm_inn) is also able to boast two famous followers in, Vanilla Ice and Kathy Lloyd.

The Wee Sheaf

James Emmerson, Camblesforth Selby

This is The Wee Sheaf pub shed, and it was named so, as I used to have a pub called The Wheatsheaf, where I had five great years and where I was able to make many new friends. My pub shed is a smaller version of my old pub, hence the word 'Wee' which also means small. Everything in my pub shed is small - apart from me, and of course the sizes of the drinks. My pub shed is also a place to relax, have fun, talk and reminisce. Everyone is welcome at my pub shed, and it is located in a small village called Camblesforth, Selby which is just outside York. My pub shed is also 8 x 8 feet in size.

The Wheel Inn

Chris & Mark Stokes, Walsall West Midlands

Around fifteen years ago my dad (Mark) saw one of our neighbours pub shed; this then gave him the idea to get one of his own. So, he set about clearing out an old shed that had been in the garden since they moved in, and he converted it into his first ever pub shed; he used an old dresser to create a bar and shelves, which he then filled with glasses; he also added a cooler with beer on tap coming out of a pull which he had been given. However, this pub shed wasn't the one he wanted, it served a purpose for a while but it was minimalistic and didn't have much going for it. So a few years later he then decided to buy a new shed; he decorated it with pictures, put a shelf up with more glasses, put up a second shelf to act as a bar and again had beer on tap; the only problem was, the new shed was smaller than the last one, and only allowed one person to fit in at any time. So, with this second attempt still not what he wanted, by the time it came to looking into creating the third shed I was eighteen and old enough to help him. So in 2013 we moved our summer house across, and we bought a 14 x 10 foot shed which we put at the bottom of the garden. At last we had a massive shed, and now came the time to create our best pub shed thus far. We then went straight on eBay, whereby we were able to purchase, a bar with foot rest, a fruit machine, real pub table and stools, a dartboard, snooker table and old mugs. We also bought many alcoholic beverages so that we could use the bottles as decorations, and gradually we have built the shed up and decorated it to create what we have today, a warming, welcoming and fun place to drink and socialise, as well as listen to music on the juke box.

243

Wifey Mac Beaties

Russ & Julia Thompson, East Yorkshire

Wifey Mac Beaties is a traditional style pub shed located near Snaith in East Yorkshire. This pub shed has been made and fitted out with reclaimed materials. Our pub shed also has the luxuries of a dart board, a log burner and plentiful supplies of homebrew from the Wifey Mac Beaties brewing company. Our pub shed is 16 x 7 foot in size and it is also quite cosy, with regular northern soul and Ska nights in the back room

THE **PUB SHEDS UK** A-Z

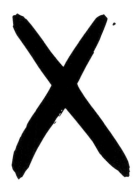

As you can probably understand, finding a letter X for our A-Z was quite the struggle, as put simply… nobody had named their shed anything beginning with this letter. So, what's the next best thing? Well, how about a pub shed that begins with a number… but not just any pub shed, an award winning pub shed which has won pub shed of the year, not once, but twice!

3 Steps Bar

Gary Logan, Ayrshire

Welcome to the smallest 'Pub' in town, the 3 Steps Bar, voted pub shed of the year 2010 and 2013. This 10 x 8 foot outbuilding looks like any other garden shed, but, on closer inspection, the 'free hut' sign on the door provides a clue as to what lies inside. The name came about because you can only take three steps in any direction., and the idea for the pub shed itself came about over some drinks with mates, and he began saying how great it would be to have a pub in the garden, and then he thought, *"what's stopping me?"* so two years ago he bought a standard 10 x 8 foot shed, insulated it and then lined it with MDF, before putting down a carpet and building a 5.5 foot bar. Gary raised the outlay of £650 by selling his Xbox, camcorder, laptop and camera on eBay. Since then Gary has spent a fortune on improvements and pub paraphernalia from around the country including a brass footrest which came from a pub in Plymouth, along with a last orders bell. In the pub shed there is also a fruit machine, dartboard, sound system, heating and optics; the 3 steps is also linked to Gary's house alarm. Gary said that *"The best thing about it is that it looks like any other shed from the outside but inside it looks and feels like a proper pub"* he also said *"My wife's the best for allowing me to build it in the garden, but I thinks she's just glad of the peace and quiet when the lads come around, because the girls get the house to themselves."* Occasionally there is also a girl's night in the pub and the lads stay in the house… buts that's rare. There is a great atmosphere inside the pub shed, whether it is a Saturday night, knocking back shots or a Sunday afternoon watching the football, they have also had a few race nights for local charities. The bar also has a dozen regulars and wherever they go they take their sheds flag with them so that they can take photos with it on their travels. So far it has been taken to Amsterdam, Benidorm, Afghanistan, America, Japan, Australia Niagara Falls, The Three Lions pub shed in England, and Barcelona, with a climb up to Ben Nevis on the cards soon. Gary has also said that he feels some people think it is unsociable to drink in a garden shed, but he says it's the opposite. There is also a strict 11pm curfew, and they recently donated £211 to the Ayrshire Hospice and £225 to Click Sargent thanks to the collection tin that they keep in their bar. They also hope to raise money for Help for Heroes in the future.

THE *PUB SHEDS UK* A-Z

The Yorkshire Kipper

Paul & Donna Batham, Altofts West Yorkshire

The Yorkshire kipper is located in Altofts, West Yorkshire and is 10 x 7 foot in size, plus an outside grill pit area. This pub shed was built in February 2015 and it is owned by Paul and Donna Batham. The shed was named after their son Charlie, who did nothing but sleep for the first 10 months after being born and he got tagged with the nickname, Mr Kipper, which has stuck. It's a sports themed pub shed, with lots of emphasis on Yorkshire, English and British themes. The bar has over 500 bottle tops under the glass top, most of which have been consumed on the premises. Football, Rugby and Boxing are also often on in the shed, and the shed seats 5 people comfortably. Joined to the front of the pub shed is a BBQ area and an outside bar that seats 3. It's also often used for family parties and get togethers.

254

Ye Old Grove Inn

Mark Allgrove, Romford Essex

Hi pub sheddies, I'm Mark and our little pub shed is located in Romford Essex. We called our pub shed Ye Old Grove Inn partly because of our name 'Allgrove' and also because of my boys always taking the mickey out of my age. We built our pub shed, because… who wouldn't want a bar in their garden? After having the shed built we astonished ourselves, because we are a family not known for DIY; so, we're proud to say that apart from getting some advice we did everything ourselves (with supervision on the electrics) the décor was an idea from a lovely country pub in Essex; Tracy and I were having lunch and we both said at the same time "This is how we want our bar!" we even took a couple of photos. Obviously it cost more than we thought it would, but we made cutbacks; my son Kyle made our saws which are hanging on the walls and the sign which is hanging outside; we learnt that when you see something on eBay or Gumtree, you can probably do it yourself. Our best bargain was our Guinness mirror, which we paid £8 for from Brick Lane flea market, as well as some other goodies which were nice and cheap. We only finished our pub shed in the last weekend of July 2015 so now it is the time to enjoy it; and no doubt my two sons will in the future. I would just like to thank my wife Tracy and my two sons Kyle and Connor for all their help making it my favourite place in the world.

THE *PUB SHEDS UK* A-Z

Zee Garage Bar

Matthew Bradley, Wincobank Sheffield

Zee Garage Bar was established in December 2013 after a conversation with my fiancée Amie. *"what would you like for Christmas?"* she asked, I replied *"I'd love to start making my own beer"* so I looked into it but the all grain and hop version looked too complicated for a novice like me, and I put it to the back of my mind. Then, on Christmas day I opened my presents and there was a beer kit in a tin with everything I needed, and it looked so easy to do. I then got to work on the brewing, and after it was brewed I thought I would love a hand pump to pull my pint with, so that I could get a nice creamy head like in the pub. I contacted Angram and got a cask pump and mounted this on to a sideboard; my first garage party was then born. It went down really well, however Amie not being a real ale drinker said *"what about making a cider?"* and then my father in law Steve said *"what about a lager?"* my in laws Alex, Steve and Charlotte then bought me a lager kit and I made my first lager. I then moved onto a pear cider, and I purchased a Carling and Strongbow pump to dispense them. However, I then realised that I had to start work on a bigger bar with my birthday money. More parties were then hosted and Jamie said, *"You should have more of each drink just in case one runs out!"* so, I did. I created a couple of each and bought more pumps, and nearly two years later we are serving three real ales, three ciders and a lager with plans for all grain brewing coming at the end of this year. The name for my pub shed came from the location of my bar, and it has stuck ever since. It has been one of the most expensive hobbies I have ever had, but seeing the smiles and enjoyment on friends and family's faces when they come over, makes it all worthwhile. I would like to say a big thank you to Amie my wife for getting me started and for putting up with all the noise, and the time I have spent in Zee Garage Bar.

Zola's Shed End

Terry Jones, London

Zola's Shed End originally started out as a shed that someone was getting rid of via a selling site on Facebook. In order for me to acquire the shed, I had to go and help take it down along with my brother in law. When I finally got the shed home, I put in a new window, which was one that my brother in law was getting rid of. I also put in a new door that someone had left in their garden; alongside this I put in two dormer windows that I had taken from my daughter's old Wendy house. I made much of what you see myself, putting my creativity to work to create windows from old washing machine doors and a wood burner out of an old gas bottle; the wood burner also has a chimney which extends out of the roof. The floor of my pub shed was made out of old pallets in order to try and achieve the rustic look. My shed was also too small for a proper bar so instead I bought a 70's style drinks cabinet on wheels, so that I was able to move it around. Zola's Shed End also started out as a summer house, but I always had plans for a pub shed in mind, which was a bit sneaky on my part. My pub shed receives its power supply from my house, and in total it has probably cost me around £300.

THE PUB SHEDS UK A-Z

ABOUT THE AUTHOR

Christopher Mark Stokes was born on 8th January and currently resides in Walsall in the West Midlands. After attaining his GCSE's and also finishing his A-Level studies he decided to try and turn a life-long passion for writing into a career. With the constant support from his family Chris has been able to complete two novels in the fantasy and horror genres. Chris has also used his passion for art in order to create a plethora of illustrated children's books aimed at a variety of age groups, from two year olds to twelve year olds. Chris loves all things in relation to science fiction and horror. Inspirations for his work are authors such as George R.R Martin, J.R.R Tolkien, Stephen King, Clive Barker and children's author Roald Dahl. He is also inspired by illustrator Quentin Blake.

More books by
Christopher Mark Stokes:

The Distant Glimmer

The Revenant of Black Manor

The Cracks

The Firestorm Files: Amber Sky

Eventual Darkness

Dawn of the Shed

THE OFFICIAL GUIDE 2015

13711700R00150

Printed in Great Britain
by Amazon.co.uk, Ltd.,
Marston Gate.